WILDERNESS SELF RELIANCE

The ability to trap food could be a critical factor in keeping you alive in a survival situation. Knowing the types of species that can be found in the area and having a good understanding of their behaviors are two ways that you can be prepared. Then it is a matter of knowing which traps will work on which animals and knowing how to build and set them to be successful. Unless you live in the wilderness and trap on an ongoing basis, you are unlikely to master all of the skills and techniques that lifelong trappers know. Their skills have been honed from knowledge developed over centuries and passed down. There are, however, some basic concepts that will improve your odds of success. The first to remember is to keep it simple. Learn one trigger trap that can be used multiple ways and one deadfall type trap for smaller animals. Learn some basic knots that you can tie with makeshift fishing lines and snares.

IC

My Pathfinder Outdoor Survival Guides offer a simple and common sense approach to being prepared for any survival situation. If you practice the skills and techniques in this guide, you will be prepared when the occasion arises. Most important is that you develop the ability to adapt, improvise and overcome adversity by learning to use what is available to you. And that you stay firm in your belief that you CAN survive – never give up.

The Pathfinder School System®

Created as a teaching tool for my students in Wilderness Self Reliance, the Pathfinder School System represents the wisdom of the ancient scouts who ventured ahead of nomadic tribes to find fresh areas to support their community.

These "Pathfinders" had to accurately identify the perfect spot to sustain their tribes – they had to recognize the resources that would afford food, shelter, water, medicines and protection – the very same resources a person would need today.

This system is designed to introduce you to the knowledge you need to increase your survivability.

Before You Go

Most survival concepts can be broken into three basic elements (The Pathfinder School "Rule of 3's"). If you can control three elements, you improve your survivability chances:

3 main killers to most lost or stranded people: hypothermia; hyperthermia; shock.
3 ways bodies gain or lose heat: radiation; conduction; convection.
3 basic needs for body function: rest; water; food.

Dave Canterbury is a master woodsman with over 20 years of experience working in many dangerous environments. He has taught survival and survival methods to hundreds of students and professionals in the US and around the world. His common sense approach to survivability is recognized as one of the most effective systems of teaching known today. For information on Pathfinder programs and materials visit http://www.thepathfinderschoolllc.com.

N.B. – The publisher makes no representation or warranties with respect to the accuracy, completeness, correctness or usefulness of this information and specifically disclaims any implied warranties of fitness for a particular purpose. The advice, strategies and/or techniques contained herein may not be suitable for all individuals. The publisher shall not be responsible for any physical harm (up to and including death), loss of profit or other commercial damage. The publisher assumes no liability brought or instituted by individuals or organizations arising out of or relating in any way to the application and/or use of the information, advice and strategies contained herein.

Waterford Press publishes reference guides that introduce readers to nature observation, outdoor recreation and survival skills. Product information is featured on the website: **www.waterfordpress.com.**

$7.95 U.S.
$ 9.95 CAN
ISBN 978-1-58355-710-5
50795
9 781583 557105
UPC 8 84682 00505 4

Text & illustrations © 2012, 2023 Waterford Press Inc. All rights reserved. Images marked IC © Iris Canterbury 2012, 2023. To order or for information on custom published products please call 800-434-2555 or email orderdesk@waterfordpress.com. For permissions or to share comments email editor@waterfordpress.com. 2300603

10 9 8 7 6 5 4 3 2 1 Made in the USA

IMPROVISED TRAPPING– A Waterproof Folding Guide to Basic Methods for Securing Food

PATHFINDER OUTDOOR SURVIVAL GUIDE™

IMPROVISED TRAPPING

A Waterproof Folding Guide to Basic Methods for Securing Food

T0124010
IC

THE PATHFINDER SCHOOL
www.thepathfinderschoolllc.com

TRAPPING BASICS

In a survival situation, you need to do everything you can to increase your chances of finding food. Setting traps is one method that uses minimal caloric output. To be successful at trapping, you need to understand the wildlife you hope to catch. The more you understand about their behaviors, the more successful you are likely to be.

Generally, traps can be deadfalls, snares, pits or containers. You will decide which to use based on the resources you have at your disposal and the type of animal you intend to catch.

To be most effective, you should:

1. Be familiar with the type of game likely to be found in your immediate area.
2. Know the most effective type of trap for the target game.
3. Know how to set the trap leaving minimal disturbance and other signs of your presence for your prey animal.

Animal Signs

To find out what sort of animals are in the area, look for these seven important clues (use your landscape and sign tracking skills):

Tracks – footprints left behind by the animal

Dog
Cat
Squirrel
Ground Squirrel
Rabbit
Mouse

Scat – the animal's defecation

Mouse
Squirrel
Rabbit
Dog
Deer

Remains – bones and/or carcass of deceased animals

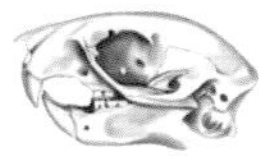

Refuse – things the animal leaves behind or remains of its food

Chewed Nuts & Plants
Browsed Plants
Squirrel Midden

Disturbance – items the animal has disturbed while travelling through or spending time in the area

Sluff – fur, feathers or other matter from the animal's body

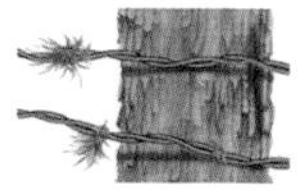

Dens/Lairs/Lodges/Nests – where the animal sleeps or rests

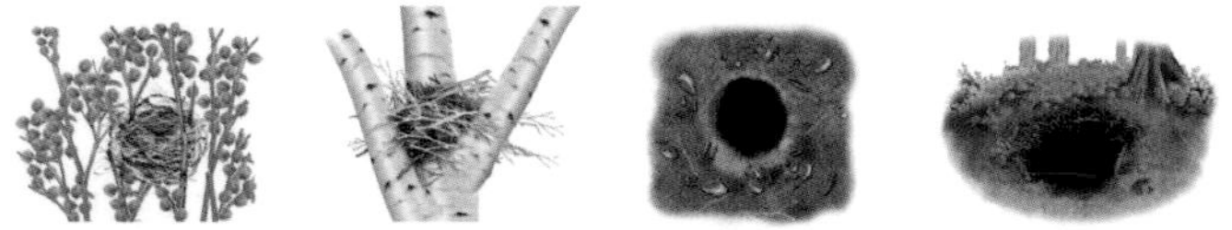
Mouse Nest
Squirrel Nest
Burrow
Den

TRAPPING BASICS

Types of Prey to Trap

All birds are edible and most are catchable either by trap or by weapon. Most mammals are edible. Small game is the best target as they are more easily trapped and much more plentiful than large game.

Survival is a self-preservation and energy conservation game – you do not want to hunt or trap dangerous or large game. There are several reasons for this: large game requires energy and weapons to hunt, time to field dress and then more time and energy to prepare the meat to eat. You will not be able to consume all of it in one meal, which means you have leftover meat to contend with – you not only have to preserve it, but you also have to protect it from other predators. By comparison, small game can be prepared and consumed quickly using all remains to bait more traps.

> **TIP** If you find scat with berries or a distinguishable food source in it, locate the food source to find clues about the species.

Trap Location Strategy

Animals need the same things we need: water, food, and shelter. Travel routes to and from these areas are the best locations to seek your prey. In choosing where to set your traps, the 80/20 rule applies. 80% of animals in an area will travel only 20% of their territory on a daily basis. Most animals will travel on high ground when moving through an area to feeding and sleeping areas, so watch the ridges for trails. Some animals, such as ground squirrels, marmots, gophers and groundhogs, use holes or lairs. Animals living in or near water, such as beaver or muskrat, build their homes nearby.

If there is vegetation that will support small mammals (nut, seed and grass eaters such as chipmunks, squirrels, voles, mice and rats), you will likely have two choices for trapping – either the small animals themselves, or their larger predators (snakes, birds, coyotes, cougars). Don't forget about water-based food sources – frogs, turtles and fish are good choices near rivers, streams, wetlands and lakes.

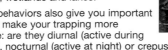

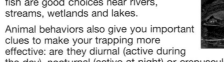

Animal behaviors also give you important clues to make your trapping more effective: are they diurnal (active during the day), nocturnal (active at night) or crepuscular (active at dawn and dusk)? This affects the time of day you should set and check your traps.

Once you have identified the types of animals you intend to trap, your next priorities are to determine where to set your traps and what sort of traps you will build. Trapping is a percentage game – the more traps you lay, the greater your odds of success.

WIDESPREAD ANIMALS YOU CAN TRAP

These are some animals that you are likely to trap or catch successfully. Learn their distinguishing features so you can identify them (be sure you can tell the difference between a frog and a toad – many toads can be toxic and are to be avoided).

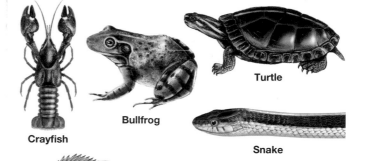

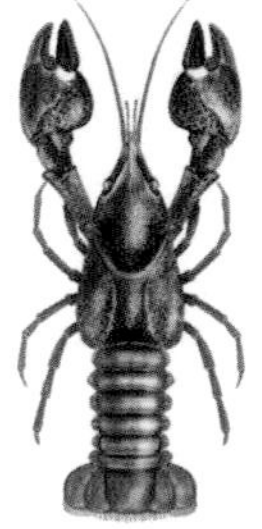
Crayfish

Bullfrog

Turtle

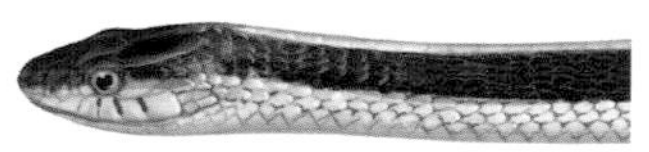
Snake

Bluegill

Trout

Crappie

Catfish

Chipmunk

Deer Mouse

Rabbit

Note: Rabbits are relatively easy to snare but cannot be a long term food source because they lack essential fats to allow us to digest their proteins.

Red Squirrel

Ground Squirrel

Mourning Dove

TRAPPING STRATEGY

Whenever Possible, Bait Your Traps

Animals will be attracted to a baited trap because they usually locate food by smell. Any time you catch food, keep the discard for bait. This may not attract the exact prey you are hoping for, but it will attract raccoons, opossums and rats – all viable food sources. An un-baited trap or snare is dependent on good luck – a bet you don't want to rely on in a survival situation if you have a choice.

Grasshopper

Caterpillar

Grub

Beetle

Toad

Fruit or Nuts

Choosing Bait

Bait is what I call a "lower food chain resource" and can be waste parts from an earlier kill (guts, skin, bones), animals that are easily captured but only partially edible (such as crayfish, frogs, worms or insects), or fruit and nuts, depending on what you are trying to trap. If you are near water, there are many bait sources available to you. If you are using non-animal bait, choose brightly colored fruit or nuts. Remember when trapping that bait will often dictate which animal is attracted to your trap, so in most survival situations expect that your catch will likely be scavenger animals.

The Strategy in All Traps Is to Funnel the Animal to the Trap

Since animals usually will follow a trail or take a path of least resistance, place your trap where they are likely to walk, and place it in such a way that it is difficult to avoid the trap. Remember the percentage rule – don't set 2 or 3 traps, set 10 or 20 and you may catch one good meal a day.

Be Aware of Contrast and Movement when Setting Your Traps

Just as searchers will be looking for something out of the ordinary patterns in nature to find you, animals are using the same observation skills to notice if something is amiss. To trap an animal, you need to be sure that your bait is noticeable and that the hazard elements blend in with the surroundings in order to make the trap approachable.

How to Clean a Fish

The easiest animal to clean is a fish; simply slice open from anus to throat and scrape out the guts with your hands. Clean the cavity with water. Retain guts for bait.

How to Gut Squirrels & Other Small Mammals

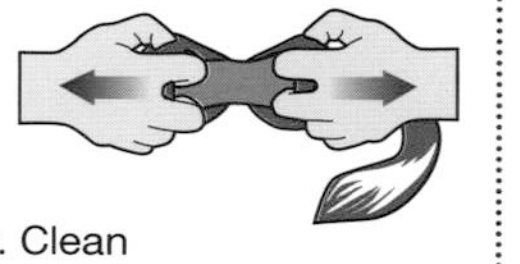

1. Cut through the skin on the middle of the back.
2. Insert fingers under the hide on each side and pull both pieces off.
3. Slice the animal open from the anus to the neck and scrape the entrails out. Clean carcass thoroughly and retain guts for bait.

How to Field Dress a Dove or Quail

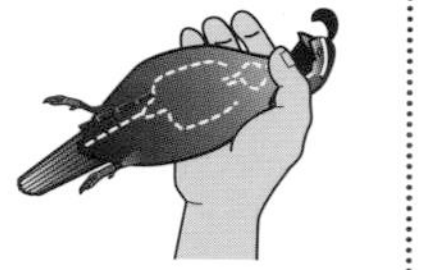

In one hand, hold the bird's head with your thumb. With your free hand, make a slit from the vent to the breast bone. Reach in and scrape out the guts, craw and trachea (windpipe).

TRAPPING EQUIPMENT

Your basic survival kit will contain some sort of cordage. To anticipate trapping needs, the best things to carry are latex or bungee-type engines and multi-ply cordage like Tarred Bank Line that can be broken down to lighter weight fibers for trapping small game or fishing. A few 12" steel fishing leaders are great ready-made snare loops that can also be used for fishing. It is always good to add several hooks and a few sinkers to your kit to add versatility for fishing. Carrying the Tarred Bank line as part of your cordage mix will eliminate the need for fishing line and can also serve for equipment repairs and construction.

Paracord or bank line can be used to make snares, traps and fishing line. Simple gorge hooks are easy to carve from a sliver of wood. Bait can be found in any rotting log, under rocks or from any waste from an earlier meal.

In a typical survival kit or day hiking bag you cannot afford the weight or size of modern metal traps. Even metal cable snares normally used for trapping are heavy in addition to other gear and should be avoided for short term survival kits. You can however, carry some very small and light-weight items that will make very efficient traps. You should also learn simple net making and cage building techniques that allow you to catch fish, birds, and mammals alive.

Remember that actual size of any trap component is dictated by the quarry you are trapping. Components for smaller animals should be sized down.

Unfortunately anywhere you travel in America trash can usually be found, but don't disregard these items as they are viable resources for traps. A simple plastic bottle cut with the funnel reversed can be very effective to take small fish and crayfish.

Trap Sets

There are 3 main types of trap sets. If you understand triggering systems you can adapt these, depending on your situation and the game you are likely to catch.

Blind Set/Trail Sets

Usually set on a travel route with the hope that an animal happens into the trap while passing down the trail. These traps should be located on specific trails used only by small game.

Baited Sets

Used to lure the game to the trap by placing bait in or on the trapping device to attract an animal from a distance. These are usually set just off the trail or in water (in the case of fish traps and some mammals).

Den/Lair Sets

Set at the entrance, exit, or both, of a den or lair. These traps, whether or not they are baited, are some of the most effective traps to set.

TRAPS

Trap Components

There are 3 main components to every trap:

The **Engine** operates the trap; this can be as simple as gravity from a falling object (deadfall) or as easy as a bungee cord or latex band tied to a tree (activated snare). It can also be a bent sapling or counterweight device but these are not always conveniently located exactly where you want to place a trap. Once you have an engine, you need to construct or carry a few triggers and lever. Knowing one or two good trigger and lever systems that can be adapted for various trapping situations will make your life much easier.

The **Lever** counterbalances the bait/trigger stick and the engine. This may be the top half of a triggering system as in the breakaway trigger.

The **Trigger** or bait stick is the component that activates the trap. It can be baited or non-baited.

Breakaway Triggers

Breakaway triggers are easy to construct from any straight green stick for many trapping and fishing situations. Find a green branch approximately ½" in diameter and 4"-6" long. Make opposing cuts half way through the stick approximately 1"-1 ½" apart and break the stick to create 2 pieces resembling chairs that match when put together. At this point remove some material and sharpen one of the "chair backs" to eliminate friction on the trigger side.

Pressure Trigger and Lever Systems

A basic toggle lever and pressure trigger is made from 2 separate components. In this case the main component is the toggle lever. This piece can be made from any straight stick that is tied either on or off center within the snare line and held in place by a fork or looped stick pounded or buried into the ground (the pressure trigger). This system can be adapted to many traps and will work for mammal, fish and turtle traps.

Deadfall Traps

A deadfall is a heavy rock or log that is tilted on an angle and held up with sections of branches (sticks), with one stick serving as a trigger. When the animal moves the trigger, the rock or log falls, crushing the animal. Deadfall traps rely on gravity to drop a heavy object like a large rock onto the prey animal as it attempts to steal the bait. Most deadfall traps are not immediate killers; the majority of animals will succumb to suffocation, but you should always be prepared to have to finish the job when you check deadfall traps.

A deadfall device needs to be 5 times heavier than the intended prey.

TRAPS

The breakaway trigger system is best for use with deadfall traps, and can be varied to be effective for different game animals. Note: the delay in the drop once the trap is triggered should be considered when establishing how high to set the deadfall – you need enough clearance for the animal to go to the bait, but the deadfall device needs to be close enough to actually make contact with the animal before it can escape. A 30 degree angle is the best bet for deadfall traps, any more than this can result in the escape of the animal prior to being trapped.

The **figure-four deadfall** is a popular and simple trap constructed from materials found in the bush (three sticks with notches cut into them, plus a heavy rock or other heavy object).

Also popular, and easier to set, is the **Paiute deadfall**. The trap consists of three long sticks, plus a much shorter stick, along with a cord or fiber material taken from the bush to interconnect the much shorter stick (sometimes called catch stick or trigger stick) with one of the longer sticks. The deadfall is a rock or other heavy object.

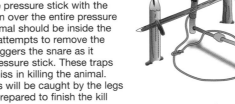

Deadfall Cages

Built to catch game, such as birds, alive, these simple cages are built by stacking opposing sticks in "Lincoln log" fashion to increasingly stretch a cordage frame. The breakaway trigger system is very effective with this trap. Use trip wires in the corners coming forward to the trigger for trapping birds, with the bait or seed placed in the center to require the animal to hop over or duck under the trip wires, which activates the trap.

Pressure Bed Traps

Pressure bed traps are normally used for blind sets in trails; they can also be baited and used as a dirt hole-type set. Dig a trap bed slightly larger than the area needed to set the pressure stick and toggle. Make a snare or net purse (if you intend to catch a bird). Place the bait on or below the pressure stick, then pad the stick with opposing sticks to create a pressure plate. Place the snare loop or a net over the pressure plate, and camouflage the trap.

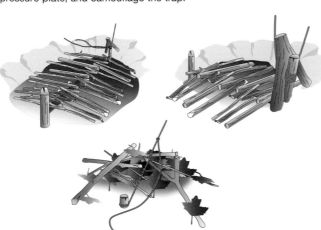

TRAPS

Baited Snares

Snares are anchored cable or wire nooses set to catch wild animals such as foxes and rabbits. Snares are one of the simplest traps and are very effective. They are relatively easy to make and set in large numbers. A snare traps an animal around the neck or the body and tightens around the animal, restraining it.

Snares are generally set off-trail so non-target animals do not activate the trap by mistake. A simple pressure lever and toggle is best for this, where the bait is placed on the pressure stick with the snare loop lain over the entire pressure stick. The animal should be inside the loop when it attempts to remove the bait, which triggers the snare as it moves the pressure stick. These traps are hit-and-miss in killing the animal. Some animals will be caught by the legs or body; be prepared to finish the kill when you check the trap. Alarming these traps in some way is a good idea, this can be accomplished with a tin can and rocks attached to the engine, so that you know when the trap has been sprung.

Fishing Traps

Both lever and trigger systems can be used to create a fish/turtle activated trap. The only difference in this method and the activated snare is that a hook and bait hung in the water replace the snare loop. Once the fish or turtle attempts to run with the bait the trap activates and the hook is set. The engine becomes a shock absorber at this point preventing the fish or turtle from breaking the line. A steel leader can be used with this system in areas where turtles are prevalent.

Drop Lines

Drop or limb lines can be as simple as a line and baited hook tied to a branch over the water, relying on the fish or turtle to swallow the bait and become hooked. It is a good idea with this system to tie it to a springy branch or use latex or bungee to avoid the branch breaking and the prey getting away.

Round Robins

This simple and effective fishing system incorporates a loop of line strung across a creek or river between 2 trees. Lines with baited hooks are hung from the loop at intervals of 2' to 3'; the loop is then strung across the water wrapped around the trunks of the anchor trees (like an old-fashioned clothes line on a wheel). Because it is a loop, you can pull the line in and back out over the water without getting into the water, and can fish for days in a single spot.

TRAPS

Spring Loaded Fishing Snare

The spring loaded fishing snare is a land-based system that releases in a springing action under tension. Fishing line or thin cordage is hung over a bent sapling or tied to a bungee; you anchor the line using a Y-shaped branch as the base of the trap. The other end is tied to a baited hook and then suspended over a bent branch with a lever and toggle in the fishing line that is released when the fish takes the bait. This spring trap can be used for animals by replacing the baited hook with a snare lain over a trail or pathway.

Fish Trap

Create a barrel shaped container from saplings or green branches (about 1" or smaller in diameter), tie smaller pieces of sharpened sapling or branches so they face inwards with a small hole in the middle that is about 2"-4" in diameter. Close the smaller end of the "barrel container" with cordage or vines so fish can't swim out of the other end of the trap. The construction will now look like a barrel with one end closed, with an inverted cone in the open end. Fish will swim into the open end through the cone, but won't be able to back out. Secure the trap to a tree or anchor well so the trap doesn't float away.

Nets

Making gill nets is simple but time consuming if you need to make a large one. If you carry an entire roll of bank line you will have plenty for a nice sized net and all the traps you want. Simple overhand knots are used to make nets, and trapping nets can be fashioned the same way without much effort. When making trapping nets slip rings must be added to allow tightening lines to be threaded through the netting so that it closes when the trap is activated.

Nets made for trapping can also be used to make dip nets with any flexible branch.

Found Tools and Resources

A sad comment on our society is the amount of waste we find in the wilderness. In a survival situation, however, an empty soda bottle or can is a treasure. From these, you have a method of carrying or purifying water; if you have a canteen with you, these containers can be used to make cutting blades, traps or other devices. Be on the lookout for these useful discards: Soda tin; soda bottle; battery; rope; plastic bag; piece of tarp; piece of rubber; bicycle tube; leather shoe; sneaker (lace, sole); cotton shirt; hat; broken glass; piece of wire; bungee cord.

Bottle trap for fish, crayfish or insects

PRESERVING MEAT

Once you have secured meat, you may need to ration your food and save some for a later meal. These are a couple of simple methods:

Sun-dry (useful when you cannot set a fire) – cut meat into thin strips, hang on a makeshift rack, skewer on thin sticks or lay on a flat stone to dry. Be careful to watch/protect the meat while it dries – flies and bugs will lay eggs on the meat and destroy its edibility, so keep them away from your food.

Fire-dry – cut the same as for sun-drying, but use fire to speed the drying process. Keep the meat far enough away from the fire to avoid cooking it; you just want the heat to remove the moisture from the meat. Once dried, you can wrap the meat in a breathable cloth or container (don't seal it, or the meat will collect condensation and spoil). If you have to carry meat that has been cooked well, it can last up to 48 hours, but beyond that it would be considered unsafe to eat.

Drying Rack

HANDLING WILD GAME FOR FOOD

It is unlikely that you have a clean environment for dressing any game you kill in a survival situation, so these are the basics you need to know to avoid making yourself sick through poor butchering or handling techniques.

1. **Ensure the animal is dead** – Prod it with a stick. Have a weapon handy to finish the job in case it is not.

2. **Gut the animal as soon as possible** – It is important to get the intestines and stomach out of the body quickly so they don't spoil the meat. Avoid puncturing the guts or stomach of all animals to avoid contamination.

3. **Clean the body cavity as best you can** – Use your hands, a bandana or leaves to wipe out the body cavity. Keep the meat out of direct sunlight if possible, or get it over a flame to dry or cook to avoid its spoiling.

4. **Clean your hands as best you can** – This will prevent you from accidentally ingesting inedible parts.

5. **Retain inedible parts for bait** – Save this bait away from your campsite if there is a risk of attracting predators.

WILD FOOD SAFETY

1. **Never kill**, handle or consume any animal that appears slow, sluggish or sick.

2. **Don't handle or consume** brains, spinal tissues or eyeballs.

3. **On larger animals**, remove the meat from bones and cook it thoroughly.

4. **Rabbits** carry the disease tularemia, which can often be detected by the presence of a white-spotted liver. Cook rabbits until very well done to kill the germ.

5. **Organ meats** – heart, liver and kidneys – should be inspected for signs of worms or other parasites. The liver should be a deep red or purple color and have a smooth, wet surface.

6. **Many animals die from natural causes**, many do not. It is good to be wary of animals found dead, due to the fact that they may have been killed by another animal that carried rabies which can be transferred through saliva on the carcass.